MONEY
MONEY
MONEY
MONEY

Love it or hate it . . . you may not *like it*, but
you can't ever *leave it*. *Everyone* can use more
money. This little book will show and tell you
the easiest way in the world to get more
money — starting *right now* — and have
enough of it continue coming in *for the rest of
your life*.

— John Milton Fogg
Editor of *Upline*™

Money, Money, Money, Money, Money
By John Milton Fogg

Copyright © 1994, by Upline™ / MLM Publishing, Inc.
800-800-6349

Printed in the United States of America
First Edition, May 1994

Published by **Video**Plus® (817) 497-9700
Book and cover design by John David Mann

Currency collage for cover art supplied by Ed Allen, Johnny Fogg and Nicholas Mann

10   9   8   7   6   5   4   3   2   1

MONEY, MONEY, MONEY, MONEY, MONEY…

There's got to be more to life than that.

It's true, there is. But there's another truth: Things go better with money — that's just the way it is.

The great singing philosopher, Francis Albert Sinatra, said, "I've been broke and I've been rich, and believe me, rich is better." He was right.

Susan sold her diamond ring — it was her Auntie Jo's, and I sold my grandfather's 18-kt. gold Vacheron Constantine pocket watch for food and rent. We had two kids. It was Christmas. We had $100. That was all.

Today, it's different. Today, we have money.

I can get my teeth fixed now. I can go skiing with the kids. If something bad happens, I can afford the hospital bills. I can give Rachel (who's 13) $500 to blow on clothes at the mall; buy Johnny (who's eight and a born musician) a guitar; have a new four-wheel drive that gets Susan and the kids up and down the mountain in ice and snow *safely*.

I can go to Hawaii, buy a big new TV and a VCR, *always* pick up the check, and give people presents till I drop — which I just love to do.

If I die tomorrow, my wife and kids are financially taken care of *for the rest of their lives!* Think about *that!*

I am free. Free to be responsible. Free to develop myself as a spiritual person. Free to be there when my kids get home from school. Free to do my work for the love of it. Free to make a positive difference in millions of people's lives. Free to let my hair grow "too" long.

I am free to be the best I can be, because I can *afford* to be. I have money.

And I know how you can have the money you want to be the best you can be, too.   — J.M.F.

What if there were a way ...

... FOR YOU TO EARN an income in a proven, professional career:

✔ that was affordable to start . . .
✔ that gave you creative control . . .
✔ that provided you the opportunity to be your own boss . . .
✔ that allowed you to work part-time or full-time — when, where and the way you chose, with the people you chose to work with . . .
✔ that educated and trained you, too . . .
✔ that was based on a proven, duplicatable system that had already worked for tens of thousands of "average" people . . .
✔ where you could honestly earn what you were truly worth . . .
✔ and where, with a little luck and lots of work, "hitting the jackpot" was truly possible?

There *IS* a way. And this book will show and tell you exactly what that can mean for you.

Somebody Else's Story

ONE DAY, A COUPLE OF YEARS AGO, Jim and his friend from the office, Beth, were having lunch. Beth was gushing with excitement. She'd just become involved with a part-time business adventure and had great hopes for it — and she was offering Jim an opportunity to join her, too.

Jim liked Beth a lot — respected her, too, but he had his doubts about what she was into. Honestly, he didn't believe most of what Beth was telling him.

"Too good to be true," he had replied. Besides, he said, he "didn't have the time." Both good excuses — hard for Beth to poke holes in, he remembered thinking.

So, Jim politely declined Beth's offer.

Jim was a resourceful and talented guy — always able to earn a little extra income when he really needed it. He knew a lot about business and finance and sometimes he'd do a little consulting for extra cash. He even prepared a couple of tax returns for friends. He hated doing that, actually; he just needed the money.

But Jim never seemed to make *enough* extra income. It seemed like every time he had money and the pressure was off — bingo — there was a car repair that cost $250 more than he'd expected; or one of the kids went out for a new sport and there was all that equipment to buy; or there was a gift that he wanted for his wife that cost much more than he could afford.

"Such is life," Jim would say. He was a level-headed and reasonable man.

One evening, sitting at his desk at home, Jim came across the brochure that Beth had given him that day they had lunch. He decided to give her a call to see how she was doing.

Beth was really glad to hear from him — and she was even more excited than she had been when they'd met over lunch together. She told him all about her business: How much fun it was . . . The special people she was working with . . . How good she felt being her own boss . . . The free time she had now to be with her two kids.

Always a bottom-line type of guy, Jim asked Beth directly, how she was doing financially?

When she told him, Jim nearly dropped the phone.

Beth said she was earning just over $2,000 a month, working about 10 to 15 hours a week — two or three hours each day.

In an instant, all of Jim's former doubts disappeared. In their place was a burning desire to know *more!*

Beth explained. Jim listened. They made a date to get together for lunch again the next day.

This time, Jim *was* interested.

This time, he said he could *make* the time.

This time, he joined Beth in her business — right then and there.

Today, Jim is earning $3,000 a month, part-time, in his own home-based business.

Thanks in part to Jim's success, Beth was able to quit her regular job. You see, because Beth brought Jim into her business organization, she now earns a small commission on all the success Jim and his people create.

Beth's work week is only about 20 to 25 hours, with a once-a-month Saturday meeting. Although she does her home-based business "full-time," Beth prefers to say she works, "My-time."

IF THIS STORY CAPTURES YOUR IMAGINATION . . .
if you think there could be something of interest
for you here, please continue reading this book.
You'll be glad you did.

And if you are not interested . . . put this book
away in a desk drawer until late some night, when,
just as Jim once was, you're sitting there wonder-
ing about how to afford the time and life you've
always wanted — and you just happen to come
across this little book again.

The Root of All Evil . . .

DO YOU BELIEVE, AS THE BIBLE SAYS, that "money is the root of all evil?" Many people do. But for the sake of setting that broken record straight, here is what the Bible *really* says: "*Love of money* is the root of all evil." (I Timothy 6:10)

You see, it's not money itself, but your being *crazy about* money, that begets your problems. And isn't it true that nothing makes you crazier than not having enough money?

"Lack of money is the root of all evil," quipped George Bernard Shaw in *Maxims for Revolutionists*.

Do you think he could be right?

✔ At 65 years of age, 95 percent of all people who retire in the United States of America — arguably the richest country in the world — have $2,500 or less in savings.

✔ The average American earns about $20,500 a year. However, the average house costs $107,400 (more than *five times* that annual earning!); the average new car, $18,500; and the average college education costs $13,742 per year.

✔ The common "marginal net worth" of most households in the U.S. is actually a *negative;* that is, most people owe more in debts than they have coming in — just like our federal government.

✔ The threshold for financial security in the United States is currently pegged at an income of $100,000 a year or more. But less than one half of one percent of all Americans earn that much.

"The trick to money," says the title of a wonderful book by Stuart Wilde, "is having some."

The nagging and ever-so-persistent question for most people is, "HOW?"

How You Earn Money ...

HERE ARE SOME OF THE MORE ACCEPTED and conventional answers to the question of how to earn money (the only problem is, they are the *wrong* answers!):

a) Go to college, get a job, have a career
b) Small business ownership
c) Buy a franchise
d) Win the lottery

Of all the above choices, "Win the lottery" may literally be your best bet.

There are more than 22 new millionaires created every month in the state lotteries around the USA. True, the odds for winning a lottery jackpot are about 7.1 million to one. But while college and a career, small business ownership, or buying a franchise, all do have better odds for success than winning the lottery, the cost to play any of those games is a lot more than one dollar per ticket.

For a person committed to a career in science or engineering, medicine or law, or for someone looking to do research and teaching, college is still the best choice.

A college education is becoming more expensive every year, and, of course, the better the university, the more expensive tuition, fees and living costs will be.

The fact is, nine out of every 10 college graduates do not end up working in the area they majored in throughout college. With economic experts claiming we will now have seven or eight different careers in our working lifetimes, only a few college grads will ever see a return on their (or their parents') investment of $50,000-plus for their four or more years of college.

As for finding yourself in a financially secure and stable career . . . the odds *against* doing that rise daily.

"I'm struggling to make ends meet today on an income I once dreamed of making," George said recently.

Until last year, George had worked for IBM. He was very good at what he did — a marketing manager earning over $70,000 annually. Working for IBM — the company known for lifetime employment — George assumed he had a job for life.

Today, George is working for a small manufacturing company. He was laid off from IBM (along with 60,000 other employees) and after eight months of looking for a job, George finally took a sales position in another state for a little less than $48,000 a year.

Take a look at the headline stories of these major magazines:

A recent cover of *TIME* magazine asked,

"What Ever Happened To THE GREAT AMERICAN JOB?"

And from a cover of *Fortune:*

"JOBLESS! The new unemployed are older and better educated than before, and stand to be on the street a long, long time."

And from *U.S. News & World Report:*

"WHERE DID MY CAREER GO? The white-collar lament of the '90s."

More than 700,000 North American jobs disappeared in 1993. In the United States, we now lose *over 3,100 jobs every day!*

In fact, **47 percent of the companies that made up the *Fortune 500* of 1980 are no longer in operation today** — which represents a net loss of *more than five million jobs!*

Paul Zane Pilzer, noted economist and author of *Unlimited Wealth*, claims that Americans will be looking at 20 percent unemployment by the year 2000.

And Americans are not alone: it's a global phenomenon. In Japan, where lifetime employment is ingrained in the culture, world consumer electronics leader Sony has laid off *20 percent* of its work force.

Clearly, no matter what country you're in, having a career just isn't what it used to be.

Besides, no one has ever achieved financial security, much less independence, trading his or her time for money. Working for someone else, you can only expect to earn, at most, about 25 percent of your real-market worth.

SO, IF IT'S MONEY YOU WANT, why not become your own boss by starting your own small business? Here's why not:

80 percent of all small businesses fail in their first two years; 80 percent of those that remain in business will not make it past year five; and 80 percent of those who do will not make it to their 10th anniversary.

Think about it: How many 10-year-old companies do you do business with?

The start-up cost of opening your own small business is staggering. Even the most modest enterprise requires you to mortgage your home, borrow from everyone you know and love, and go way out on a financial limb just to open your doors.

That's quite a gamble for a game where only one out of every 25 will win.

When you own your own business, no matter what hours you put in, you own that business 24 hours a day. Most self-employed small-business-people average 14- to 16-hour work days — at least six days a week. In truth, most entrepreneurs don't own their own businesses — *their businesses own them!*

And as *The E-Myth* author Michael Gerber points out, most small-business-people really just *own their own jobs!*

OK, THEN WHAT ABOUT BUYING A FRANCHISE?

Franchising is a brilliant concept. A franchise dramatically reduces the risk of failure in starting your own business by providing an already proven, duplicatable business system, usually with a brand name and product people recognize and trust. For a fee, you simply buy one and go to work. Franchises are called "turnkey" businesses, because in theory, you simply pay your money, step in, turn the key, and drive away down the highway of small-business success.

Today, franchises account for more than 35 percent of all goods and services sold at retail in the United States — over $800 billion!

The average successful franchise costs about $85,000 for the fee, which does not include the cost of the real estate, the physical facility itself nor the equipment. Also, a franchisee must pay the franchise company a percentage of sales for as long as he or she owns the business — whether it's profitable or not.

Approximately one third of all franchise operators fail; one third break even; and one third make a profit.

Once again, much better odds of winning than the lottery; but then, a $100,000-plus ticket should be a *sure* thing — not just a 1-in-3 chance.

WHAT THE WORLD REALLY NEEDS is a way for people to have the best of college and a career, small-business self-employment, franchises — and, yes, a little bit of luck, too.

What if there were a way …

… FOR YOU TO EARN an income in a proven, professional career:

- ✔ that was affordable to start …
- ✔ that gave you creative control …
- ✔ that provided you the opportunity to be your own boss …
- ✔ that allowed you to work part-time or full-time — when, where and the way you chose, with the people you chose to work with …
- ✔ that educated and trained you, too …
- ✔ that was based on a proven, duplicatable system that had already worked for tens of thousands of "average" people …
- ✔ where you could honestly earn what you were truly worth …
- ✔ and where, with a little luck and lots of work, "hitting the jackpot" was truly possible?

AND WHAT IF THAT CAREER OPPORTUNITY were open to everybody; if your age, sex, education, race, religion, family background, start-up money, past success or failure … truly didn't matter at all?

AND WHAT IF you could be joining one of the fastest growing and most economically powerful developments in the history of free enterprise — the home-based business revolution?

In 1993, home-based businesses accounted for total revenues of $382.5 billion in the U.S. alone. There are 35 million home-based businesses in America today, and a new one opens *every 11 seconds!* Experts predict that 44 percent of all U.S. households will have a home office by 1995. What if you could be part of *that?*

WHAT IF advancement in this profession were based on helping others succeed? What if — instead of clawing your way up the corporate pyramid, stepping on others to get ahead through cutthroat competition or office politics—what if the more you helped other people achieve in terms of money, advancement and recognition, the more of all of those things you received as well?

AND WHAT IF you could finally earn what you were really worth . . . ? If $300 to $500 to $1,000 a month part-time, $3,000 to $5,000 and more full-time were truly possible for you . . . ?

Would an extra $12,000 a year appeal to you?

How about the real possibility of doubling or tripling your present income?

And what if the top income earners in the profession were taking home $10,000, $30,000, a month and more — some of them, much, *much* more!

Would any of that interest you?

If all that you just read were true, legal and viable, and people just like you were already doing it and succeeding — i.e., there was living proof that it could be done *and is being done* even as you read these words — would you be willing to take a closer look at it?

Well, all that you've just read *is real and true,* and as millions of people around the world are discovering, Network Marketing Sales may be your ticket to earning the money you want and deserve and providing you with the lifestyle you've always dreamed of, plus a whole lot more!

The Profession of
Network Marketing Sales

First, let's take a look at what Network Marketing Sales is NOT.

NETWORK MARKETING SALES IS NOT AN ILLEGAL PYRAMID SCHEME.

Actually, there is nothing inherently illegal or un-ethical with a "pyramid shaped" organization. Here's why, according to Dr. Karl Dean Black:

"... *Above a certain size, any organization that distributes products or services ends up shaped like a pyramid, with multiple levels that get bigger as you go down. Delegation creates a multi-level pyramid. Our government is also a multi-level pyramid. So are our schools and churches. All successful businesses, because they distribute products and services, end up shaped like a multi-level pyramid.*"

Dr. Black goes on to point out that the real "pyramid" issue is one of *value*.

"Our government distributes services down a pyramid, but we give it power from the bottom, with our votes. Marketing companies distribute products down a pyramid, but we give them power from the bottom, with our dollars. So pyramids set up a flow that runs two ways: first down, then up. Value flows down the pyramid; power in response flows up. If value stops flowing down, power (in the form of dollars or votes) stops flowing up, and the system collapses."

An example of an *illegal* pyramid scheme would be a Ponzi scheme — a money merry-go-round based on stealing from Peter to pay Paul. An example of a *legal* pyramid scheme is Social Security — paying out benefits earned yesterday to recipients today with tomorrow's money. In both cases, as long as money continues to come in, it can be paid out. However, when the income stream stops, the out-go does, too — and from then on people lose.

Network Marketing Sales is like neither of these.

In 1979, Network Marketing Sales was proclaimed a legal and viable method of distribution and sales in the U.S. courts (FTC versus Amway,

23

1979). Rules and Good Business Practice guidelines were established and all legitimate Networking companies adhere to these standards and practices.

NETWORK MARKETING SALES IS NOT A "GET-RICH-QUICK" SCHEME.

There *are* examples of people who have "hit the jackpot" in Network Marketing just by being in the right place at the right time — but they are rare. More common are examples of industrious men and women who have grown successful full- or part-time, home-based businesses through consistent effort and years of persistence.

Can you get rich in Network Marketing Sales?

Absolutely. This profession offers the most level playing field of any career opportunity. What that means for you is that everybody in Network Marketing Sales has an equal opportunity to earn the highest incomes possible. Unlike any other career or profession, the *only* limitations in this business are self-imposed.

There are no "glass ceilings," no barriers to race, age (with the exception of minors under legal age) or experience. Network Marketing Sales is a truly equal self-employment opportunity.

NETWORK MARKETING SALES IS NOT TAUGHT AT HARVARD BUSINESS SCHOOL (NOR STANFORD, NOR OTHER COLLEGES AND UNIVERSITIES).

Why not? Because Network Marketing Sales is a powerful *alternative* to the conventional college-and-career track; we're "the competition"! And frankly, Network Marketing Sales is just not "college material." Not that it's not a worthy subject—it's just too simple. Even a beginning Networker can teach you the fundamentals of this business — certainly enough "how-tos" to get solidly started earning income and building a sales Network—in a single afternoon!

NETWORK MARKETING SALES IS NOT A CAPITAL-INTENSIVE START-UP.

You can get started in Network Marketing Sales for as little as a few hundred dollars of product inventory and marketing materials to help promote the products and the business opportunity.

With an investment of a few thousand dollars, you could have all the inventory and marketing materials you require to start a number of your new associates in business *and* completely furnish and equip a fine home office!

NETWORK MARKETING SALES IS NOT A DISTRIBUTION BUSINESS.

Contrary to what some new people think, Network Marketing Sales does not require you to stock substantial inventory and distribute or deliver orders. Most Networking corporations today cut out the costly middlemen and distribute their products directly to the consumers for you.

The amount of product inventory required depends solely on the intent and scope of your individual Network Marketing business plan. Samples to show and tell with, products for your retail customers, and initial inventory for your new associates is usually sufficient and commonly costs just a few hundred dollars.

In Network Marketing Sales, you *are* responsible for marketing and selling the products and services and providing "customer service" support. That's what you are paid for.

NETWORK MARKETING SALES IS NOT AN EMPLOYER/EMPLOYEE RELATIONSHIP.

In Network Marketing, you are the owner, president and CEO of your own business. You are a self-employed, independent contractor who signs an agreement with your chosen Network Marketing Sales company to represent the company's products or services and build your own Network Sales organization and adhere to the company's policies and procedures.

Network Marketers *do not* work FOR the company; you work WITH the company. The business relationship is a tangible and dynamic partnership where the company provides:

the products and packaging, research and development, capitalization, financial management, legal and regulatory compliance, data processing and IMS (Information Management Systems), administration, order taking, the creation and production of marketing materials, purchasing and production, quality control, product satisfaction guarantees, warehousing, shipping, associate services, field and leadership training, incentive programs, etc.

— and your role is to provide the marketing, sales and end-user customer support.

Considering the scope of each partner's contribution, it may seem that the company is doing the lion's share of the work. However, because 80 percent of a company's success depends upon effective marketing — *and if there are no sales there is no business* — your role as a Network Marketing Salesperson is vital to the profitability of the company. Which also explains why you can be so richly rewarded for your successful business-building efforts.

NETWORK MARKETING SALES IS NOT A BUSINESS WHERE INCOME IS EARNED FOR RECRUITING.
No ethical or legitimate Network Marketing company compensates its associates for the act of recruiting. In Network Marketing Sales, you are paid ONLY on the products you sell and you earn commissions on the sales generated within your own Network Sales organizations.

Which leads to taking a look at some of the things Network Marketing Sales *IS*.

Networking Marketing Sales

First and foremost — it is what its name implies. Networking and Marketing and Sales.

NETWORKING
One of the buzzwords of the '90s, "networking" is defined in the dictionary as:

an informal system whereby persons having common interests or concerns assist each other, as in the exchange of information or the development of personal and professional contacts.

In Network Marketing Sales you do both of these: you exchange information and you develop personal and professional contacts.

However, in this business, the "network" system has been made formal:

1) By rewarding you for exchanging information that results in product sales; and

2) By enabling you to build your own Networking Sales organization from your personal and professional contacts and to earn income from

the successful efforts of your Network of business associates.

MARKETING

All of the creative work that goes into a seller offering a product to a buyer is marketing. In Network Marketing Sales, the company itself provides much of the promotional material used by their sales associates, as well as training on what to do; how that material is *used* and *presented* is the individual associate's business — literally!

Simply stated, marketing at its best is *making an offer people can't refuse.* Traditional marketing would include advertising, merchandising and promotion. In Network Marketing Sales, we accomplish our marketing goals directly through personal, individual word-of-mouth marketing.

In Network Marketing Sales, you market and make offers for two things:

1) A product (or service).
2) A business opportunity.

In Network Marketing Sales you have the ability to earn income by buying products at wholesale, reselling them at retail, and pocketing the difference, which is your *profit margin*. Retail sales are referred to as "right now money," because Network Marketing Sales is a cash business. You will pay cash for your product purchases, and your customers will do the same with you.

By successfully marketing the business opportunity, i.e., having new associates enroll into your own Network Sales organization, you are able to earn commission income on the sales productivity of the group of independent business people you enroll, manage and train.

SALES

All businesses must sell something — and just as marketing is the creation and communication of an offer, sales is *the successful completion of the transaction.* Since no one earns money in Network Marketing Sales *until* the sale is completed, sales is the "make or break" element in both the Network Marketing company's and the individual Networking associate's success.

Networking companies choose the unique method of Network Marketing Sales to accomplish two primary selling objectives:

1) To get their message to consumers whom they would not be able to reach through advertising, merchandising or other methods.

2) To introduce those consumers to products or services and opportunities they otherwise wouldn't know about.

Only by achieving these two objectives will the company accomplish its goal of sales.

Now, you may be uncomfortable with the word "sales." If you are, please, consider the following questions:

✔ What are preachers and teachers, if not *salespeople?*

✔ Have you ever been *sold* on having something in particular for dinner . . . on watching a particular TV show . . . on going to a party . . . on listening to a piece of music or reading a certain book . . . ?

✔ Were you to comfort a frightened child who woke up from a nightmare about a wolf under the bed by assuring the child that everything was okay . . . would that not be *sales?*

✔ Is there anything you own and value that someone *sold* you?

✔ Are you married?

From one perspective, much of life — and much of what we value and even cherish in our lives — has been made available to us via sales of some kind.

In Network Marketing Sales, selling is the process of creating positive relationships based on *the exchange of value* — whether that value is achieved through buying your products or joining you in your business opportunity.

In Network Marketing Sales, the form of selling which works best is person-to-person, educational selling — giving customers and potential business associates *an informed choice.* In fact, consumers today *demand* such an educated choice. They will not settle for the hype and hustle of days gone by.

Here is what *Unlimited Wealth's* Paul Zane Pilzer said in a recent interview in *Upline*™:

"Network Marketing Sales today holds THE GREATEST PROMISE OF ANY MARKETING INNOVATION for accomplishing the goal of educating consumers about new products and services."

What that means for you is that more and more, people will be turning to you as a Network Marketing Salesperson to learn about new products and services they want and need, yet don't know about *yet*. Clearly, the kind of educational sales done in this business is very powerful!

The kind of *sales* which people object to is the arm-twisting or hyped-up selling approach of the con-man — the person who takes our money, but does not give us fair value in return.

That kind of sales *simply doesn't work* in Network Marketing Sales, because this is a people-people business built upon a foundation of integrity and positive personal relationships.

Since any relationship based on manipulation is doomed to fail eventually, selling of the kind just described above *destroys* one of the most unique and extraordinary advantages of having a Network Marketing Sales career — the possibility of earning RESIDUAL INCOME.

The Secret of the Wealthy...

RESIDUAL INCOME IS SIMILAR TO ROYALTY income, such as that earned by a successful author, musician, songwriter or inventor, or the dividend income earned from investing in stocks or real estate.

✔ An author or musician creates a book or song one time, but then earns a small percentage of every copy of the book that's sold, or every time the song is played on the radio or sold on a record, tape or CD.

✔ An inventor invents a device and then receives a small percentage of the sale price every time one of his or her manufactured inventions is sold.

✔ An investor purchases a stock or buys real estate, and receives dividends or rent for the financial life of that property or investment.

In each of these illustrations the person invests his or her initial time or money — or both — and then sits back and collects residual income off the continuing sales, dividends or rent from the asset he or she created for the life of that product or investment.

A person who earns residual income can actually walk away from the daily affairs of his or her business, secure in the knowledge that the income will continue. In Network Marketing Sales, there are countless examples of people being away from their businesses for extended periods of time, returning to find that their incomes had actually increased!

Residual income is the secret the wealthy of the world have known *and kept a secret* for ages. They need not have bothered — for unless you were blessed with the talent to create a best-selling book, hit song or better mouse-trap, or you had the excess capital to invest in solidly performing stocks or appreciating real estate — there was no real opportunity for you to participate in earning residual income.

But now there is.

Network Marketing Sales enables anyone, even those of average means, to build a business that generates the kind of lasting, residual income that wealthy people enjoy.

If the product or service you represent is *consumable*, and of such value that a significant number of people will continue to buy and use it for years — then Network Marketing Sales will provide you with residual income.

If the product or service you represent is *durable* — i.e., not consumable — but your company develops and produces a continuous stream of highly desirable new products that consumers value and continuously want to own — then Network Marketing Sales will provide you with residual income for years to come.

With the right products and a company structured and managed to sustain the business and grow long-term, the possibility exists for you as an independent Network Marketing Sales associate to create and continue to generate residual income—earnings you get paid long after your initial efforts to create them have been completed — and there is the genuine possibility to continue doing that *for the rest of your life!*

You can see another unique aspect of residual income by looking at it in terms of *asset value.*

Ask yourself, what amount of money in the bank or invested in stocks or real estate would it take to have a dependable and continuous income of, say, $5,000 a month?

At today's rates of return, that would require a capital asset value of approximately *three quarters of a million dollars.*

If you, as a Network Marketer, were earning $7,000 a month or more — which is quite achievable for a full-time effort, even after just a few years — you would for all intents and purposes be living *like a millionaire!* And you'd be doing that without the need to literally earn a million dollars — nor would you have all the hassles and responsibilities that come with it!

One desire you may have right now is to see exactly how this income-earning process works in Network Marketing Sales.

Here's how.

How You Earn Money
In Network Marketing Sales

FOR OUR EXAMPLE, LET'S USE A NETWORKING
business opportunity based on a consumable nutritional product that helps people lose weight. But truthfully, whether your product is *consumable,* or *durable* — such as consumer electronics, educational or environmental products — or *a service* — such as financial instruments or telecommunications — the principles of building a Network Marketing Sales organization all work pretty much the same way.

And to put you in this picture, let's say you represent this product line through your own Network Marketing Sales home-based business.

STEP ONE: USE THE PRODUCTS YOURSELF
Become your own best customer. With a product that gets the results you want and represents real value, this should be easy to do — wouldn't you agree?

Once you have learned how to use the products yourself — and let's say you pay $50 per month for the products at your wholesale cost

(Network Marketers purchase products at a discount from their companies for their own use and to retail to others) — you now simply go find two other people who are interested in getting the same benefits you've gotten and sell them your products.

And that's Step Two.

SECOND STEP: RECOMMEND THE PRODUCTS
You now have two retail customers — and by the way, these are probably not strangers you need to sell on some difficult "cold call"; these are people you already know. They're two of your family members, friends, or associates to whom you've recommended the products because you knew they would like them and benefit from them. You did that just the way you would recommend a great new restaurant you discovered, or a new movie you saw and loved, which they haven't seen yet.

Perhaps you recommended your products to six or even a dozen people before you found those two who were excited enough to try them. In this way, in Network Marketing Sales, the more people to whom you recommend the products, the more people you will have buying them from you.

And please consider one more very important thing: Every legitimate Network Marketed product comes with a 30-DAY MONEY-BACK SAT-ISFACTION GUARANTEE. And this clearly works in your favor, as well as in theirs: any time you sell someone your products, there is no risk to them at all. If they don't like them, for any reason, and even after using the products for 28 or 29 days — if they do not get the results you promise, you can give them their money back with the confidence that your company will fully repay you. No one ever loses. Does your local supermarket, drug or department store make such a guarantee?

So, you have your two retail customers who do the same thing you do: they purchase $50 worth of wholesale product monthly. As long as the products perform — and good products will continue to do so — you've established a business base of $150 of sales volume per month. Now, it's time for Step Three, which is simply to teach other people to do *what you have already done yourself.*

STEP THREE: SPONSOR
In Step Three, you go out and find three people like you who are interested in earning extra money from a part-time business that can generate lasting residual income.

Again, there's no need to talk to strangers. Have these "opportunity" conversations with the people you already know. And much as you did in recommending the products, you may have to talk with a number of people before three of them say "Yes" and want to go into business with you.

Remember what happened in the beginning of this book with Beth and Jim.

Once you find your three people who want to build their own Networking businesses, you simply teach them to do what you already know how to do: Buy $50 worth of products themselves each month for their own use; and through word-of-mouth, personal recommendations to people they already know, have two retail customers who do the same thing. This will be as easy for them to accomplish as it was for you.

In Network Marketing Sales, this process of recruiting or enrolling new business associates into your sales organization is called "sponsoring." And now you have the simple, yet powerful, One-Two-Three Step formula for doing this business successfully:

1) USE the products.
2) RECOMMEND the products to others.
3) SPONSOR associates into your Network Sales organization who do the same thing.

And remember, when you bring someone into your business, he or she is also the President and CEO of his or her own business, just as you are. It really is an inspired breakthrough in the free enterprise system!

Now, back to your business-building process.

With your three new sales associate/business partners doing the same thing you have done, you now have a total monthly sales volume of $600 — your $150 plus $150 in sales volume for each one of the three of them. Again, you simply teach them to do what you have just learned how to do; and that is, show them how they can generate a monthly sales volume of $600 each.

When your three associates have each reached a sales volume of $600 per month — which you have worked closely with them teaching them how to do — you (and your Network organization) are producing a total volume of $1,950 (their $600 in sales each, which equals $1,800, plus your $150).

Now, you'll teach them how to do that, too.

> **Remember, all you are ever doing is teaching your associates how to do what you already know how to do. Because this business is built on your simple duplicatable effort, that's all you will ever have to do in Network Marketing Sales.**

The next level of your and your group's sales volume totals $6,000 a month, and once again, after you've achieved that, you teach your people how to do the exact same thing.

Incidentally, $6,000 in monthly sales volume will propel you into the leadership ranks of most Networking company's compensation plans. What that means to you is that you're now being paid a higher commission on your sales as well as qualifying to earn extra bonuses, such as car allowances, travel benefits and additional incentive income, as well.

The next volume level you and your people achieve would be over $18,000. And the next, well over $50,000. And the next . . .

Can you see where this is going?

An Example

USE		Your Total Network Sales Volume
Buy $50 of product for your personal use		**$50**
RECOMMEND		
Find 2 people who do what you have already done	2 x $50 = $100	**$150**
SPONSOR		
Find 3 people who do what you have already done	3 x $150 = $450	**$600**
Help those 3 people do what you have just done	3 x $600 = $1,800	**$1,950**
Help your 3 people do what you have just done	3 x $1,950 = $5,850	**$6,000**
Help your 3 people do what you have just done	3 x $6,000 = $18,000	**$18,150**
Help your 3 people do what you have just done	3 x $18,150 = $54,450	**$54,600**
Help your 3 people do what you have just done . . .		

Now, let's be bottom-line, much as Jim was with Beth: What does all this volume mean to you in terms of your personal income?

Most Network Marketing Sales company's compensation plans pay commissions of between five and 10 percent of your and your group's wholesale monthly sales volume. With a monthly sales performance of $50,000 in wholesale sales, that would mean you could be earning between $2,500 and $5,000 per month, or from $30,000 to $60,000 annually.

Not bad at all for a part-time effort — an effort based solely on each individual involved doing something anybody could do: simply consuming $50 of beneficial products each month, and finding just two other people to do the same thing.

Consider these two questions for a moment:

✔ Can you imagine having such a great product to offer, yet sharing it with only two people — *ever?* That's the total number of people to whom you've recommended the product in this example.

✔ Can you imagine having a product that gets such great results for you that you look and feel better than you have in years — and no one notices? No one ever thinks to ask what you're doing?

Honestly, to have *no more than two* people know about your products, you would have to work very hard at keeping them a secret!

And with an opportunity to earn an annual income of $30,000 to $60,000 or more from a part-time, home-based business, where all someone has to do is learn something simple, do it him- or her-self, then show just three other people how to do the exact same thing — well, just try keeping *that* a secret!

The Next Step In the Evolution of Free Enterprise

NOW, WHY WOULD PEOPLE BUY PRODUCTS from you or another Network Marketer, rather than from a retail store or mail order catalog?

Good question.

For the answer, let's turn to the best-seller, *The Popcorn Report*, written by Faith Popcorn — a woman who predicts the major consumer trends shaping the future of business for *Fortune 500* companies.

(If you're not familiar with the term "cocooning," Ms. Popcorn created it to describe the major consumer trend of more and more people choosing to stay at home, safe and secure, having food delivered, watching videos instead of going out to the movies, home-based business programs, etc.)

Here's what she says:

"The home cocoon will be the site of the future shopping center. All members of the family will be able to shop from one location. Instead of going to the

store, the store will come to us, no matter how unusual the product or how frequently needed. On our [computer and TV] screens, we'll be able to hear about the latest new products or styles, or order up our old favorites.

"Like the corporation, the shopping experience as we know it has grown cumbersome, inefficient, a violation of the trends. The big department stores are discovering that it's no longer possible to be all things to all customers. The shopping center is becoming a dinosaur in the grand scheme of things.

"Today's mail-order catalogs and sale flyers (piled up in the house somewhere waiting to be thumbed through and discarded) are obsolete — too much wasted paper, plus the post office is too inefficient, postage too expensive, to keep sending them through the mail.

"The means of distribution will be the next consumer-oriented revolution. Direct shopping from the producer to you — bypassing the retailer altogether, no middlemen, no stops along the way."

The only thing Ms. Popcorn didn't mention was what marketing experts have discovered: that in purchasing a new product or service, *95 percent* of the decision is based on the personal recommendation of a friend or associate.

You see, people don't trust big corporations or their advertising any more. They trust other people. That's why, as Ms. Popcorn asserts,

"Instead of going to the store, the store will come to us . . ."

The most introverted and shy person you know will, when thinking about buying a new car, walk up to a total stranger in a parking lot, say "Hi," and ask, "How do you like your . . . (such and such)?" We do it all the time.

What's Possible For You
In Network Marketing Sales

CAN YOU SEE NOW JUST HOW EXTRAORDINARY and powerful Network Marketing Sales is?

Network Marketing Sales has become the fastest method of new business expansion in the world! That's why people are calling it "the next step in the evolution of free enterprise."

Here are the names of just some of the prominent, international *Fortune 500,* NYSE and even Dow Jones corporations currently involved in Network Marketing Sales *because* they see its marketing and sales power — *and* because they know their futures depend on it.

Gillette, Colgate-Palmolive, Sprint, MCI and AT&T, Fuller Brush, Amway, Firestone, Rexall, Avon, Primerica, IBM, GM, Toyota, Service-Master and others . . .

But, as we said, people don't particularly trust big corporations any longer. We trust each other. So, here are some real people — with names and faces — whose personal stories are the most persuasive arguments of all to encourage you to seriously consider a career in Network Marketing Sales.

 TAMMY THOMPSON wasn't looking for a business of her own. In fact, she really didn't want to work at all — but she had to. Tammy's husband, Rick, was in the military. They lived off-base and all the money they made went for food and rent. Their third child, Chase, was just five months old. Tammy had a job in an insurance office. She cried every morning going in to work.

"Everyone in the office weighed over 200 pounds," recalls Tammy. "We just sat there all day long and ate doughnuts."

No matter what Tammy did — and she *did* try everything — she just couldn't lose weight. She was huge, tired and depressed and "Just Over Broke" (which, Tammy says, is what "JOB" stands for).

One day, one of the agency's customers ran in to pay her premium and Tammy noticed her loose-fitting clothes were literally pinned on. Tammy asked the woman, Josette, what she was doing, and Josette dropped a bunch of brochures on Tammy's desk, saying, "Call me if you find anything interesting there."

Before Josette got to her next appointment, Tammy called her on her car phone and told her, "You get back here right away. Whatever it is — *I want it!*"

After she had used Josette's products for only two days, the other women in her office already were commenting on the positive difference in Tammy. They, too, wanted the products right away — and before Tammy knew it, she was in business for herself.

"The products just took over," Tammy says. "I didn't know what was happening. Within three weeks, my retail profits exceeded what I was making selling insurance!"

Tammy's new business enabled her to leave the insurance office in less than a month; her success enabled her husband Rick to leave the military and join her in their Networking business. Today, Tammy and Rick earn a six-figure annual income.

"I can't think of anything I could be doing right now that would give me the satisfaction, the income, the freedom, happiness, enjoyment and fulfillment that Network Marketing Sales is giving me," Tammy says. "There are so many women who are strapped in jobs that keep them away from home, away from where their heart is. They need to go for it — and Network Marketing is absolutely the best way to go."

JIM KOSSERT still wakes up at 4:30 in the morning, a hold-over habit from his days as a commercial fisherman. Today, though, Jim never has to "go to work" ever again. The residual income from his Network Marketing Sales business is approaching $150,000 *a month!* He does it, very simply, because he loves it.

"Here's a great test of whether or not you're really happy in your work," Jimmy says, "You just answer this question: 'If I could afford it, would I do this for free?'

"My answer is — *absolutely!* I love this business!"

Like most tremendously successful leaders in the Network Marketing Sales profession, even though he and his family are financially set for life, Jim Kossert still works hard. "But I play hard, too," he adds.

"This is a fun business," Jim says. "It's the only business in the world I know of where you can go out and help people get what they want . . . and also change their lives for the better . . . and in the process, get all that you've ever dreamed of and more.

"There's so much power in this business," Jim adds. "Leverage is one aspect. In any other profession, you're paid only for your own efforts — and sometimes you can be paid handsomely. But the trick is to do what J. Paul Getty meant when he said he'd rather make one percent of 100 people's efforts than 100 percent of his own.

"Building a Network Marketing Sales organization enables each of us to do that. It's as if, instead of being a one- or two-income household, you're a 500- or 5000-income household — and that's incredible!

"I obviously value my own freedom," Jim concludes, "but I've got to tell you, when you're responsible for creating freedom for other people, that's the greatest feeling in the world — and the more lives you touch, the greater you feel. It just keeps getting better!"

When GEORGE RUIZ first got involved in Network Marketing Sales, he was broke, his car had been repossessed, and George was forced to sell his TV and microwave and borrow money from one of his brand new Marketing Associates in order to buy products for his first three months in the business.

"Actually, I don't feel the money was a challenge," George says. "When you have a commitment, money is not a problem. My biggest challenge was that I didn't know *how* to work the Network Marketing Sales business."

So George went on a crash course to learn all he could about the business. He read all the books and listened to all the tapes he could get his hands and ears on. "Even if you learn just one idea," George says, "that alone can pay for all the books and tapes you have." In addition, George's sponsors actively partnered with him to help him build his business.

"Even though you're in business for yourself — you're not all by yourself," George says. "That's one of the special things about Network Marketing Sales."

Although George earned $50,000 last year, the money isn't what George values most about his successful business. "It's the freedom," he explains. "And only when you experience that for yourself, only then do you realize what Network Marketing Sales is really all about.

"Last summer, my two daughters wanted to go out for softball. So, Monday morning, I took them down to the ball field to practice. My six-year-old son went with us and he looked around the field and asked, 'Dad, where is everybody?' I told him, 'Well, everybody's working.' And that's when I realized the tremendous freedom I have to be with my family, to have my life be what *I* wanted. Freedom is the most important thing this profession gives you."

 Ten years ago, JAN RUHE was just coming out of a very nasty divorce. Although she won custody of her three children, she was faced with over $100,000 in legal bills and she didn't know how she was ever going to pay them.

"I knew I couldn't go back to a 'normal' job," Jan said, "but I owed all that money and I had these goals of sending my kids to private school, buying my son a baseball uniform, and I wanted Sara to have a little white fur coat and black patent leather shoes."

Jan looked at addressing envelopes from home, baking cakes (but she hates to cook), "I looked at everything, *everything,*" she says. Then she discovered Network Marketing Sales. Within eight months, she had accomplished those initial goals — and a lot more besides.

"I wanted to earn $100,000 a year more than anything in the world," Jan says. "And I was floored — *absolutely floored* — the day I realized that I'd already made a million dollars in my career!"

Jan is now a leader in Network Marketing Sales. She's a top producer and the top producer of leaders in her company. She's earning $200,000 a year and is well on the way to earning her second million.

"Nowhere else but in America and in Network Marketing Sales could I have the opportunity — especially as a woman — to earn $200,000 a year or more," Jan said. "And while money's not what it's all about, it does buy you the freedom to move. Financial independence has been a tremendous relief to me.

"Network Marketing has enabled me to make a difference in the lives of thousands of women. That's a high for me: that I've been able to unlock the vault and give people the torch to fire up their own dreams, to fulfill their own ambitions, and not have to settle for being average anymore."

BOB WALLER has a degree in marketing as well as a Masters in banking and finance. For seven years, he was president and CEO of both a savings bank and a successful Savings & Loan.

"But even after 16 years in the banking business and achieving all my career goals," says Bob, "I found I was *still* vulnerable, dependent on other people, at the whim of regulators, etc. — even as the president and CEO! So, real financial independence was what I wanted most.

"In the beginning, my generalization about Network Marketing Sales was negative," Bob admits. "I thought it was a pyramid scheme or some home party thing. I didn't feel comfortable with either of those. So, I began really looking into it.

"With my background," Bob says, "I had to feel comfortable with the marketing and sales technology; plus, as a banker, I evaluated the profession as I would any financial investment — assessing the risks, judging the returns. The result: I became enamored with the concept of Network Marketing Sales."

Soon Bob was earning a strong five-figure monthly income; "a lot more," he says, "than I ever did at the bank —no matter how profitable we were.

"I can pretty well assure people that Network Marketing Sales will fulfill their goals, and — if they are teachable, have the desire, and are committed to the process — they will achieve whatever level of success they design for themselves. The only thing I can't assure them is how long it will take.

"You know, it's true," Bob said. "The only people who don't succeed in Network Marketing Sales are the people who quit. Do you know of any other profession or career where if you just stick with it, you'll be a success?"

THIS LITTLE BOOK STARTED with "Somebody Else's Story," and it has ended with five stories of ordinary men and women who are all living extraordinary lives, just because they became involved in Network Marketing Sales.

All that's missing now . . .

. . . is your story.